Breaking Through

Poems by

Carol Leavitt Altieri

Goose River Press
Waldoboro, Maine

Library of Congress Card Number: 2021944602

ISBN: 978-1-59713-238-1

First Printing, 2021

Cover and interior art by Rachel Schumacher.

Published by
Goose River Press
3400 Friendship Road
Waldoboro ME 04572
e-mail: gooseriverpress@roadrunner.com
www.gooseriverpress.com

Dedication

Hope is the thing with feathers
That perches in the soul
And sings the tune without the words
And never stops at all.

— Emily Dickinson

For Frank Scot and Michael Altieri
and Grandchildren: Jacob, Alyssa, Lianna, Hannah,
Michael Jr., Mason, Marciano, Mia and Isla

And in Loving Memory:

Frank Anthony Altieri, April 11–October 18, 2011
Alicia Ann Altieri March 4, 1962–August 8, 2008

Contents

Part One

Contents

Part Two

Special Thanks

Many grateful thanks for the creative and artistic illustrations and designs for the poems by Rachel Schumacher of Schumacher Creative Design and her cover painting. She was a joy to work with and helped solve printing guidelines. The cover by Rachel beautifully illustrates many of the poems.

In addition, I appreciate the hard work of Deborah Benner, Goose River Press, accepting my poetry for publication. Her technological, printing abilities, time and expertise have been invaluable.

I am indebted to the Guilford Poetry Guild Members who have encouraged me and have allowed me to open up and to go deeper into writing my poetry. They have helped shape my poems profoundly and more artistically.

I would like to thank all the poets in the CT Poetry Society for helping me bring the poems into their final forms. Sincere gratitude to all who gave encouragement and stimulated me in many ways and who have been unfailingly helpful.

My abiding thanks to Edwina Trentham for being a poet of wonder, for stimulating ideas, offering suggestions and strong creative support as the poetry book took shape. I enormously appreciate her gifts of thoroughness and originality planted in my poetry.

I shall always remember my debt to my first poetry teacher in graduate school at S.C. S. U., Dr. Vivian Shipley, who keeps the creative spirit and its messages of love alive. She started me on this journey and helped my poetry grow with passion, complexity and imaginative leaps.

Much continual appreciation to Jennifer Payne for excellent publishing/ promotion of the Guilford Poetry Guild and for keeping the web site so very stimulating and up-to-date.

Part One

Our Community of Dairy Cows

Over flowing rivers after spring rains
and the scent of new grass,
in the first light of day,
I unhitch cows' stanchions.

Holsteins and Guernseys
trail out of the barn
their milk bags swaying.
I bring them to water
and grass, talk to them,
delight in their thick hair,
pink noses and long-lash eyes
that stare directly into mine.
Some nuzzle their calves
and want to remain with them.
Heads bobbing, calves sticking close
they are spooked by our border collie.

Calves bawl for mothers,
mother cows mooooo for calves.

A coyote waits alone by the stone wall,
perhaps thinking about snatching
a calf or a young heifer.
Some cows watch the coyote and run
toward it until it disappears.

Our cows bring me in tune
with the land and cycles of their lives.
From shy to bold, of different personalities,
they live in the barn at night
along with the raucous geese
and scolding roosters.

I embrace this blessing of knowing cows,
this holy vessel of memory.

Our Community of Dairy Cows

Oak Tree Monarch

Across the road from the red barn, the oak tree reigns
on the granite uplands of our East Andover farm.

In Spring, the canopy unfolds with Baltimore orioles
and warblers that skip and flit from branches to ground.

In summer, near lichen soft nest, hummers
with rapidly thrumming hearts glow like flying jewels.

Under its shade, 1 smell the fragrance of grass
at dawn and hay at dusk.

Eating another apple from the orchard
I love to ride the tire swing as high as it will go.

In the fall, I climb to a crook in the oak and build
a secret club house to invite friends.

At night, I look into its branches through my window
hoping it protects me from witches and evil spirits.

After high school, I leave my mark on the tree
and trek away to find a new age
of adventurous possibilities

Oak Tree Monarch

Black-Capped Chickadees in Madison

For months, no birds came to the patio by the pines
until one day the temperature drops to a frigid 12 degrees.

I look and listen in astonishment and delight
when a black-capped chickadee, a paragon of its kind

sings sounding like "Sweet Weather!" and "Spring's Coming!"
calling chickadee-dee-dee-dee!

I scatter a feast of sunflower seeds
and other cheerful birds land—

along with woodpeckers, nuthatches
and some tufted titmice.

A whole flock flies in all taking turns and not squabbling,
grab seeds, land on branches

eating the fruit inside.
Another waits its turn and flies in

fluffing up its feathers, turning its head to look at me.
Then many more black caps decorate

the white birch tree branches.
All the travelers congregating here illuminate

the pandemic year
with gladness of companionship—

all symbols that winter will soon be vanquished
and spring, the life-changing season can begin.

Black-caps in Madison

Hunger Drives Evolution

In the North Carolina forest
you happen upon a Venus Fly Trap,
a very unlikely encounter
with a plant rarely seen, cloaked in a tangle
of bull briar and honeysuckle.

Covered by pearl dew drops
and glass facets of lime green and rose.
In summer it offers a drink of narcotic nectar,
interlaces trigger leaves with slippery sides.
Its chambers catch a hawk moth or a caterpillar,
or a spider that changes its color to match the leaves
or an ant that dances into its clutches
and escapes, telling about its find and inviting
other ants.

Other times, a caterpillar makes a life-long home
or a wasp sculptures a nest inside.
The plant masquerades, evolving tricks, increasing its libido.
Instinctively, this pitcher plant's primitive instinct
is to move; thrive on digesting corpses.

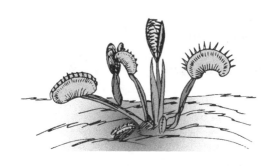

Hunger Drives Evolution

9

Japanese Cherry Trees — Sakura

In spring the suite of exquisitely
flowering cherry trees with pink
to rose blossoms emerge from
winter's doldrums. They form
a canopy overhead —
spreading
their drooping branches
from reddish-purple bark.

The people of Japan celebrate
the heavenly trees
with graceful-artistic hanami.
Artists come from all over to paint
an interplay of motifs.

Cloaked in blossoms
children dress as interlocking flowers
in rich reds, spring greens
and vibrant yellow kimonas.
Families and friends enjoy
parties of sushi, ramen, tempura
and famous dishes as takoyaki*
and okonomiyaki*

Drinking sake,
they continue through the night
bathed in an ethereal glow
chanting
"these petals fall when
they must just as we do."

Lucca Biodynamic

In Tuscany, just beyond
the medieval walls,
country villas and pastures,
biodynamic vineyards flourish
free of chemicals,
in Arcadian slope of greenery
where donkeys graze
in the labyrinth
of tangled paths.
Rosemary, lavender and rosebushes,
exhale bloom
intoxicating and pulling us in.

Wildflowers and white blossoming
olive trees blanket the terrain
in honey-colored gardens,
purple clover, golden mustard flowers
and crimson, wine vines,
a different dynamic way of growth.
The Lucca Biodynamica,
at center of all, Giuseppe Ferrua.
Swallows, honeybees and plants thrive.

In 1735 Baroque Chateau
in sylvan hush,
we taste wines, made with natural yeasts,
that express their territory.
A deeper flavor
determined by heavenly bodies,
harvest under a full moon
mirroring the tides.

11

Lucca Biodynamic

Hidden Wounds of War

Two truck bombs struck buildings in Lebanon
killing members of a peacekeeping
mission. My dead buddies cut me deeply.
The spread of attacks and terror
convulsed, rose up inside, compelled me
to sign up with the Marines
against my mother's advice.
(My father a retired marine stood by me.)
The letting go, my head shaved,
my individuality stripped away by drill instructors
and I was recast into a man who earned
an elite place in the Marine Reconnaissance.

When deployed to Afghanistan
a suicide bomber truck packed with explosives
launched into a campground killed hundreds.
Improvised land mines, helicopter blades
mangled bodies.
Men on stretchers-the blood, the deep flesh tears,
the disfiguring burns
the need for oxygen, the end of breath;
other grave wounds of war traumatized me.
I had to come home and console families
storing wounds and deaths in bone-deep memory.

I signed with a Rapid Deployment Task Force
and promoted: won a Silver Star, Bronze Star,
and Legion of Merit.

When I came home my wife and two children
welcomed me from that mountainous road;
I fought invisible battles all the time,
and suffered acute depressive attacks.

After a year home, I was sent
back to Afghanistan,
as commander of a Second Battalion
called the Magnificent Bastards,
yet I couldn't command any more

Wounds of War

It's Complicated

Under a luminous sky,
he suns his shaved head
and hairless golden body.
His brow squints, he rolls
his eyes and smirks
when I ask for the loan
pay back.

Like a wandering albatross,
he uses dynamic soaring
and gets a free lift.
He looks at me
his face confident, like a frigate bird
gives a withering look
turns away — needing to deflect.

When I give him my poetry book,
"I never read books."
Yet, he tells stories, sharing narratives
of his life with four brothers
and marine reconnaissance pictures.
"I have a fourth degree black belt in karate
as my father had,"
and he is afraid of ants and spiders.

Guarded in studying his networks
like the Sopranos, he keeps his secrets.
Perhaps the Desert Storm Battle
still influences him.
To me, hope and despair compete
neck and neck.

Landscape of Change

When I smell crab apple blossoms,
I see a yard in a country town
and my sister climbing a tree, lofting
in its branches not knowing its meaning
in time. Barn and tree swallows open
their wings and inscribe messages on the air.
I, river tripping, follow the tributaries where
belted kingfishers swoop across and lunge.

American bitterns thunderpump from patches
of sedge. On muddy, meandering banks, spruce
trees, conifers and trilliums give way
to a grove of trembling aspen.
I keep my past in the present realm and garden
to have our songbirds and frogs return.

Landscape of Change

17

Beloved Adino

I was once terrified of dogs
nearly lost my life to a wire- haired terrier.
On a sweltering August Day,
he tired to bite my leg off
rolling me over the ground —
as his fearful mistress brandished a hoe.
I was scarred for life.

And I remember our first dog Buffy
who bit children as they rode their bicycles
by our circle
and had to be put away, hopefully to dog Heaven.

Life was OK without a dog.

Until my teen-age son smuggled
a mixed golden- haired puppy
into the basement, making a house for him
telling, "Don't bark! My mother
doesn't want you here!"
Reluctantly, I was able to rise to accept
the new dog.

When my son grew up and left home,
Adino became my confidant, teacher
and extra-treasured friend.
When I suffered and struggled
with an actively broken heart,
he gave me unwavering gales of love.

Beloved Adino

Part 2

His golden-white fur shines in the sunlight
when I take him for a walk.

He charms the friends we meet in the park
and quivers with happiness when they pet him.

Adino senses when I'm going away in the car jumps
in and curls up in the back seat.

In the fenced cemetery, I play with him
throw a ball for him to catch and return.

He enlarges Frank's heart, who never owned
a dog. Love does its work....

Once he climbed on the school bus and
went to school with Alicia.

Then, Adino turned twelve
suffered from arthritis and vertigo,
and had to be carried upstairs.

He depended on me to navigate for him—
awakening and howling at night.

We were each other's mutual saviors
until his ghastly, whimpering death staggered
me.

I cant foresee owning another dog
—no one could replace him. I still feel the
pleasure and pain rising inside me.

Milford Track

For years now, I've wanted to trek
this ancient trail,
repository of Maori history.

Calls of sea birds echo
over cliffs of granite, tectonic years of life
resting on top of one another,
a sacred place where heaven
touches earth, vistas fringed
with thousand-year-old kauri
trees, coniferous branches
climbing all the way up the trunks
opening into a crown.

North from Lake Te Anau
to Sandfly Point on the Sound, I tramp
over mountain passes, up switchbacks,
cross flooded creeks as four seasons
in a day carve the crevices.

Above the falls, silver-eyed bellbirds
spill music as they plummet
to catch coral salmon. Alpine thunder
and boulders crunch together,
crash down mountains.
Wingless takahe and purple swamp hens
flee from hunters.

High above crosses stand on fjord ridges
where others before us have fallen.
I cross the stepping stones on the river.
Mountain gentians hug the rocks
away from scathing wind.

Suns slanting light mixed
with mist from mountain lakes
echoes the silent evensong
of the spheres.

Butterflies Rock the Block

--Tribute to Joy Soybel*

Joy pushed against the boundaries
of the newly manicured wilds of Del Webb
and carved out land from Juniper Landscapers
for a butterfly garden.
She expands the choir by calling for others.

Volunteers plant passion vines for Gulf fritillaries
and milkweed plants—staking the cages;
covering them with white mesh bags.
Before they finished, two butterflies came,
symbols of hope for the new land.

A swallowtail and monarch hang around
hovering over the plants. They flit
from one plant to another and bask
in the sun on the flat rocks.
On my morning's walks I look at the covered plants
looking like Casper the ghost and his many friends.*

A Galaxy of Worlds, Boreal Conifer Forest

Come join me as I venture north
to the vast boreal, spruce forest of Canada.

A multi-hued wilderness of majestic creatures,
named after Boreas, Greek god of the north wind.

Winging out of a hawk's nest of a spruce tree,
Great Horned owl, enhanced in frosty plumage

with golden lit eyes and large brown ear tufts
swoops down and grabs a startled skunk.

One of the strangest birds, the Boreal owl
keeps hunting red-back voles — even when not hungry

storing many extra ones in crevasses of trees,
incubating corpses when needed.

We can see the smallest Elf owl, the size of a sparrow,
fly out of the sweeping coniferous forest.

Hear the multitudinous voices of winged creatures
and see the boundless snow and partly frozen lakes.

Amid the vast sweep of permafrost
thousands of tundra swans ascend in a bird blizzard,

having completed their journey from northern Canada.
Other emblems of the boreal: woodland caribou,

grizzly bears, elk, and the Siberian tiger
in all its beautiful design — call this place home.

The Roman goddess of the dawn, Aurora Borealis
shines her glory over all announcing the coming of the sun.

Columbia's Quindío Wax Palm Trees

The forests once controlled
by Revolutionary
Armed Forces of Columbia,
a place visitors
couldn't go then; guerrillas etched
threats in waxy bark.

On the other side of the valley,
open pit gold mines threaten
the Wax Palm Preserves.
Reserve palms are marooned in pastures,
some seedlings die in full sun —
or are eaten by cows and pigs.

Light- colored trunks are coated
with a thick wax.
Leaf scars make dark rings
around the cylinders.

From the river basin of the Andes
two striking toucans with gigantic bills
hop on the outstretched palm branches.
Dark green and gray crowns breach
into hazy clouds.
I stand below looking up
into 10,000 feet elevations
with trees cascading down mountaintops
heartened by their beauty and lushness.

Sun on branches illuminate a host of birds:
toucans, parrots and jays- land and sing,
pulled in by orange red fruit.
Voices are in discord.

Columbia's Quindío Wax Palm Trees

Watching Three Blue Leviathans

In the ocean of Iceland,
I'm sharing my breath
with the most massive
and mysterious animals ever to have lived.
Weightless under the sea,
they live twice as long as my fellow humans.

Suddenly, blue whales swell out of the sea
like albatross.
A trumpeting blast, a thunderous tone
burst and blow of pluming water.
Dorsal fins rise.

Then three, matriarch leading, bolt out
of dark green and bluish water
finding their own way.
Bigger than a school bus with jaws as high
as an oak tree,
tossing back tons of tiny krill.
Resembling a work of art, translucent,
silver bright,
reflecting rainbow colors.

Once as frequent as moonlight,
now living on the knife edge.
With the fishermen we hear
whooshing sounds of breathing
and hauntingly beautiful,
complex sounds.
They improvise the intricacies
of diverse, distinct melodies.
Viewing their world through echoes,
they send coda clicks to one another.

I hope they rebound from the curse
and mercy of our civilization
so our children can know
their majesty and awe.

A Geyser Erupting at Yellowstone National Park

...I know not why I am so sad,
It wearies me, you say it wearies you.
But how I caught it, found it, or came by it,
What stuff tis made of, where it is born
I am to learn.

— The Tempest: Act 1, Sc .1

A young adult, you were
our Grand Prismatic Spring
and we couldn't bear you going away
by yourself.

Still, you flew across the United States
to work at Yellowstone the summer of 86
and I later heard
hitchhiked to your destination.

We drove west from CT. to visit you.
Our hearts were brimming, looking at
Old Faithful,
landscape of mud pots,
steam vents
and rainbow-colored hot springs.
Together, we loved: rich blue tones,
kaleidoscopic colors, bubbling surfaces
and swirling streams.

Decades later, I return
walking alone to see
Yellowstone transformed from
the dreamscape,
our prelude to tragedy.
Flamed by Yellowstone, I am reminded
of the sharp grief of losing you.

A Geyser Erupting

Deacon Grave Native Wildflower Walk

Out wandering, morning sun lures me
on this pandemic day. The scene
pulls me in to an old-fashioned wildflower
garden-in keeping with 1759 farm house.
Boxwood and holly hedges mark
the garden border;
an aura of serenity shelters me
with only a police car
nearby keeping watch on some linesmen.

Plants crowd along the wooded path,
shadowed by sugar maples
and blossoms of the ancient oaks and tulip trees.
All along the path, pearl whiteness shimmers,
purple violets harmonize
and lapis lazuli hepatics open stars of beauty.
Red-brown trilliums
or Stinking Benjamin unfurl
slightly drooping with their heady scent.
White bloodroot
with deeply-lobed leaves appear
from leaves that encase the petals.
In fallen leaves, hundreds of flowers
with pink, purple petals grow.

Deacon Grave Native Wildflower Walk

Dutchmans' breeches
hold heart-shaped leaves.
White Butterflies land on blood root.
Black and grey pussy willows
bring the garden alive in the town.
Beloved sky blue bells color the scene.
Silver-and-green Solomon's seals
arch around ferns
of ancient lineage flinging branches wide.
A counterpoint of foliage,
luminous pink lady slippers
intersperse with woodland plants.
Veins of gold embroider with gems of light
weaving through.
The gracious, hardy spirit
of the planters rises from the soil.
Gloom of enormous loss, fear and tears
of corona virus evaporates for a while.

Part Two

The Fightback of the Kirkland Warblers

I feel the shadow of loss,
deeply aware of the fragility
of birds depleted numbers.
Cowbirds and blue jays
once besieged them
and ate their babies
in their jack pine tree nests.
Now, with the help of humans
warblers are rebounding
lifting my heart.

During a long day's birding, I watch
the handsome male's
richly - textured bluish body
that subtly merges with dark streaks —
Van Gogh yellow belly — each wing
emphasized by a white bar.
A broken white eye ring
brings drama to its head.
He bobs his tail up and down —
singing
chip-chip-chip-too-too-weet-weet.

The female flies in with others
to the top of a pin oak tree.
The Kirkland
warblers pluck seeds and berries
after their long journey
from the Turks and Caicos Islands.

In late afternoon, the dappled sun filters
through pine trees gilding their feathers
like golden sculptures
in newly planted forest.
With beguiled eyes and ears, I see
in the distance other rare warblers
alight—forage at lower levels.
They hold forth
in an ever evolving chorus—
madcap outpourings.

The Fightback of the Kirkland Warblers

Black Birds Fly

(Kerry James Marshall's gallery show at Chicago Art Museum)

On the south Side of Chicago
    afternoon sun warms the black-top street
staghorn sumac springs from sandy soil
    of abandoned back yards where invasive weeds flourish.

Kerry James Marshall finds a lost crow out of place.
  He watches the crow soar above-land on the ground,
topple on its side, stand up, hop around, look hungry.
    He captures it and takes it home,
cuddles it in his shirt.

He ties a rope to the crow's leg and feeds him mulberries,
    paints him and then lets him go.
Later, he sees the crow being scared by a feral cat
tells the crow, "You better keep your butt off the ground
    because I may not be around to rescue you. "

In one painting a crow is too large for the birdhouse
    he tries to enter. A second painting of a grackle,
of a small birdhouse enhanced by pink and yellow blossoms.
    Cardinal and grosbeak are flying in different directions.
He says, north and south, the scene depicts the pecking order.

    One could have the thrill of birding visiting his gallery.
His art shimmers and takes flight like the crows,
    and grackles he paints.

Black Birds Fly

Hiking Along to Acadia

Hike the land to fulfill a lasting bond
with the peninsula's finger tips
where fresh water of the Sheepscot River
shimmies its tentacles to Muscongus Bay.
My father's Yankee fishing village slides out below.
Islands link out, one ahead of the other,
trailing berries of red and sea-foam bayberry.

Walk terraced steps, taste wild blue berries.
After the coniferous forest, duck under a swing bridge
and leave your pain-riven world behind.
Close to thunder hole, ocean booms
against a boulder-piled, jagged shoreline.
Barnacles feather out on intertidal rocks
and fiddler crabs scuttle to shelter in seaweed.

When sunset comes, gaze at the deep blue bay.
Listen to the water thrush's harmony
and I'll try not to leave this place of beauty
where sister and daughter, lost family I love
will be waiting.

Hiking Along to Acadia

Imperiled Rhythms of Great Barrier Reef

I dive down from Audubon's glass bottom boat.
My eyes adjust,
over the ocean's stage
of an Edenic underwater garden
where nature laid out its grandest show.
A rainbow of marine life crowds around me.
I 'm in a world dyed seaweed green and blue.
Quintessential here where time is not important
across the distance of millions of years.
A chorus of the iridescent water soaks into my skin.
Marble colored sunfish shimmer.
Sting rays ricochet and cascade startling
and warning me to move on!
A haze of blue and aqua green,
between emerald spikes,
a dragonfly munches.
Fearsome stoplight parrotfish
graze on polyps.
Some multi colored denizens allow
watchful stillness
while inquisitive green morays
and sea anemones
wield stinging arms.
A boxer crab fights off
a blue-ringed octopus.

Coral reefs created
by billions of marine organisms,
as polyps in intricate webs of cracks and cavities.
A time of transcendent alchemy envelops
as I merge with my surroundings.
Today the devil is always here
doing its harm but also
we devoted protectors.

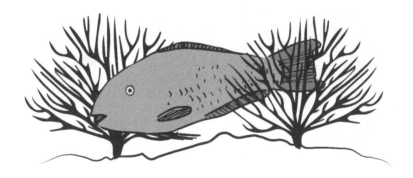

Imperiled Rhythms of Great Barrier Reef

The End of the Line

Wearing a black, rich, tailored suit
he placed his marine reconnaissance hat
on the back seat.
They met two years ago
when he drove her to the airport.
He starred in his profession of driving athletes,
governors and celebrities
around in his limousine service
and worked as a private detective
for Stephen King and Mohammed Ali.
She was gloriously grateful when he offered
her a ride home from the airport
after a European trip.

He charmed her with his story, his charisma
the confident sound of his voice
telling her about his interesting family:
Irish father, Italian mother and four brothers,
his father and one brother, state police.
He said his father had a fourth degree black
belt
in karate and raised all five sons to be men.
He had two black belts in karate too.
He captured her with his eyes
the way an osprey catches a fish.

The End of the Line

That night and morning her head on the silk
pillow
she slept fitfully with frightening dreams.
Her deceased husband once warned her
about protecting her assets.
She was held by his expressive brown eyes.
Golden skin and shaved head
anesthetized her,
awakened feelings of generosity.
Later, after a background check,
she shivered with bone-deep anxiety
and thought she had lost her way.
Still, remembering from her religion
every human being has redeeming features.

Snowball the Cockatoo Grooves

In this avian paradise
watchers look at each other
rolling their eyes.
Snowball loves to dance to Queen's
"Another one bites the dust"
supporting Darwin's claim
that animals like music.
He performs from a stage,
a site in shade from dappled sun
on the forest floor.

The fires of desire are lit—
he has his own wild moves
promises new talent in hip hop,
grooves to music in a curved path,
does contortions, otherworldly gliding,
filled with staccato bursts.

Step motion pantomime,
sways as if on a ship.
Freestyle interactions in the moment
inventive as a swing band.
A feathery bottom wiggles
poised to conquer another territory.
I want to copy his artistic swings
at Donahues.

Snowball the Cockatoo Grooves

Family

In the purplish time after daybreak in April
aboard on a Covid 19 day,
the first chipmunk weighing
only as much as a quarter
hunches down
on the blue slate steps,
stretches out his little body—
stripes of reddish brown, grays, tan
black, and chestnut.

He skirmishes from underground tunnels
of the stone wall
next to the house that haunts.
I watch from my sliding glass door.
The scene radiates, takes on meaning
with the sun coming over the shade
of the green trees.

A second, third one and fourth arrive
running in formation,
playing follow-the leader
scurrying back and forth.
A tight-knit family
doing everything together,
chasing each other
with tails held straight up
like flags.
With no grasshoppers this year for lunch
bird seed is their manna.
On the patio they give me
a stylish performance
dancing one way and then another.
As they tuck seeds into their chamber,
a downy woodpecker watches
and then tries to steal them.
Behind their squeals,
I hear my daughter's voice.

Family

Celestial Divination

After sunset in Hammonasset Park,
I trek out to take pictures of Comet Neowise.
It will be 6000 years before
it will pass again. I feel awe rising inside me.

A weird cigar-shaped flash speeds in the solar system
one of the brightest in my generation.

The astronomer directs us:
Look up at the northern sky, find the Big Dipper
and follow its ladle
10 degrees above the horizon
reaching its apex between orbits of Saturn and Neptune.

Catch the unsettling apparition
behaving strangely with a dust tail 10 million miles long;
leftovers from our solar system creation,
taking up to 20 years to orbit the sun.

A nuclear core of ice laced with rock and dust,
reappearing over and over again through centuries.

Neowise fraternizes with the rest of the sky —
crowds stars and hundreds of modern satellites.

People are enamored of viewing Neowise,
Instead of the evening news, pandemics, police and riots;

something amazing we don't have to worry about
gone to the Great Out There in interstellar space.

where stars are born.
What a spectacular nighttime show!

The solar system shimmers with Neowise highlights—
we seek refuge for our troubling times.

Celestial Divination

Star Viewpoint

Before midnight,
I go out with an astronomer from Audubon
to view the stars
vibrating in the sky.
I think of Plato who believed the stars
to be the final destination
of all moral humans
after their sojourn on earth.
In the sky I see the square of Pegasus
with four bright stars in the corners.

I imagine the North Pole where the sun
does not rise between September and March
and think of my sister and children who once
lived near there in Sweden.

The first magnitude star, Deneb
marks the tail of Cygnus the swan,
who slides down the Milky Way galaxy.
I look to the southern horizon, see the twinkling
red super- star Antares, the heart of Scorpios.
A great view of an Orion meteor shower
as earth passes through a line
of meteoroids left over
from Hayley's Comet.

Soon the moon will be at perigee
the closest point to earth
with Mars, Mercury, Saturn and
Venus appearing together.
They guide warblers migrating,
travelling nonstop
to South America and make me feel related
to all of nature and the cosmos.
All of the stars seem transcendent
connected to heaven, God
and immortality.

Starry Sky Connections

For years now
I've felt the ties that bind us,
gazing in awe and wonder
at the spectacle of stars
of the Milky Way galaxy
as our planet spins.
Along the paths of latitude,
no matter where we are
we all see the same sky
and moon at different times.
Star gazers in Eastern Europe
share the same sky with us.
The sky I see will, in a few hours,
be the same for my cousins
in California as they are
lured exotically
into the seductive moonlight.
Stargazing, too, carries us forward
and backward in time.
Hundreds of millions of years ago
those who once gathered in the fields
under the stars are still connected to me.
Looking ahead, I hope,
this same sky will enlighten
all our future generations.

Starry Sky Connections

Moon Gazing

Tonight, the friendly harvest moon appears
In all its splendor, large special and brilliant
taking on fiery colors of red and orange
with a human face of eyes, nose and mouth.

On Flag Hill farm, lightning bugs flicker
as we bring our Guernseys and Holsteins
in from the pasture for milking.

Native Americans thought wolves sang the moon
into existence calling it the wolf moon.
I'm not certain, but I believe some humans transform
into wolves when the moon is full.

I watch it move along parallel with the horizon
seeming bigger than ever as a procession of broad-wing
hawks and peregrine falcons soar over.
Golden eagles join the pass over too in front
of the moon as the lunar light shows
near St Michael's tower.
Earth and moon align perfectly as the sun
blots out the moon's reflected radiance.

Hannah Dancing to the Music of Time

The third granddaughter, born in March,
as were my beloved Alicia and son Michael.
I rejoice in Hannah's complexity.

On vacation in Ogunquit, Maine, at twelve years,
with a broken leg, she rides with feet pressed
onto the pedals of the wheelchair—laughing
and daring Jake her cousin to push her
over the curb—where she falls out.

She evokes Artemis in her charisma
and love of life—
that keeps the party going.
Sweetheart of rhythm with friends
who collectively improvise on Facebook
and Instagram. She blazes through
college years with academic acclaim
and a progression of motifs.
As a sought after friend, I imagine
her singing and dancing
moving in time with hard rock bands.
Other times, she runs up Heartbreak Hill
in the Boston Marathon keeping up
with other strong runners.

A princess of *One Thousand and One Nights*,
she creates fairy tales in whimsical kingdoms
for her niece Isla.

During college Hannah flies to Africa,
in Ghana taking wing
helping moms give birth.
My eyes have seen the glory
as she passes onto others the care ignited
by numerous warriors, men and wise women
who have embraced her.

Alyssa

Born in September, time of the harvest moon
that rises in the sky — brilliantly colored
in red and orange —
moving parallel with the horizon.
I remember when she was a toddler
wearing a red bonnet,
her father pulling her and Lianna
in a bicycle cart
during summer vacations.

I recount my memories
of my wonderful granddaughter. Now Alyssa's
on the threshold of a new venture,
an honest heart in the land of accounting
and care giving.
I admire her beauty-lapis lazuli eyes
and brown hair with porcelain skin —
body full of vivacity.

Whenever I visit, I marvel at the way
she makes my favorite charcuterie;
and serves me a glass of Cabernet Sauvignon.
She eludes sadness from losing loved ones;
allows hope to dwell.
I glimpse her face in my dreams,
hoisting a banner
an ally of the family covenant.

In her future life, she will live it
without me and our beloved Alicia,
she played with when a child.
I bequeath to Alyssa, my cherished
antique Dresden doll, grandmother
Alice gave Alicia, my daughter.

Visit With My Grandson

Near the swaying sugar maples, you discover a painted box turtle
with green frogs jumping out of our shady back yard pond.
You take my attention away from the treadmill.
The painted turtle burrows in the grass as you wheel barrow
on Grandfather's woodland gardens.

Some green frogs from Celebrated Croakers' College
close eyes to make
a leap of faith as they catapult to stardom.
One, like a Calaveras County frog kicks and springs into the air
echoing my childhood farm
at the pasture's edge years ago in Andover, New Hampshire
under blue gaze
of Kearsage Mountain.

You and I stand at pond's edge bending our heads like turtles.
You free your hand to touch one stretching his neck
to hear star frogs' songs.

Here links confide commentary.
My grandson and I marvel at woodland creatures;
woods rich with mountain laurel, swamp lilies, painted turtles,
thrushes and piping frogs.
Our measure of change and reverence
and prayer.

Integrity and Dignity from Deep Within

Oh! what captivating hearings
for Amy Coney Barrett with her Covid
mask on.
She spent three days of testifying
without any notes.
She was pelted with
questions designed to trap her
by partisan, evading senators.

Amy refused to give hints, previews
or forecasts of future thinking;
she always kept her dignified bearing.

"I can't infuse my own policy views
on the Constitution," she said.
How hard it must have been
for mother, father, husband
and children who stood by.

"We are all originalists," some said.
As the days wore on,
She wouldn't be trapped
an honest-to-God originalist.
All the players converge
and voting soon came to a head,

Ruth Bader Ginsburg
and Amy Coney Barrett
very similar in lawyerly and scholarly esteem.
I couldn't understand
the opposition to such
an accomplished woman!

I could heal echoes of Judge Scalia
and I worried many nights
about her confirmation.

Good Luck and Safe Crossing
(During the Great Amphibian Migration this year with the decline of traffic coinciding with Covid 19 the road crossers have more of a chance to thrive.)

In other years on rainy nights
a naturalist would call me
to come out and rescue
frogs and salamanders
in danger of being struck,
crushed by vehicles.
Leaving underground homes
to seek mates, they head
for a bacchanal.
Hundreds try to crawl
or slither or hop across roads
to another woodland pond.

The first miracle,
a spotted salamander
wide protruding eyes,
purple-black body
glistens with bright yellow spots.
Drunk with anticipation,
it thrashes and wiggles
across the road. Cheeks pump
to breathe. I pick one up and feel
its heart beat.

My eyes follow
the next road crossers, tiger salamanders
in patterns of yellow and black
accompanied by wood frogs
trilling and spring peepers
sounding like distant cow bells.
They carry a sense
of rich regeneration
and evolutionary lineage.

White-Breasted Nuthatches at East River Condo

In December, thankful for my favorites,
in leafless oak tree, the first one upside down
descends head first anchoring himself.
Four and a half inches, top of head midnight black
white and black eye stripe runs from bill to nape.
Body below, hued bluish-gray, upper rufous-cinnamon.
He probes for hidden larvae under scaly bark
of the old tree trunk;
applies a sticky resin to his warming home.

The second one finds a sunflower seed, hacks
it to small piece, wedges it into a crevasse
of a nearby tree.
A hairy woodpecker watches, snatches
and grabs pieces of the hidden seeds.
The nuthatch shouts "yank, yank, yank,"
like a toy trumpet.

Somewhere far away another land is calling;
some blessings remain, as I breath a prayer,
for them to stay here for the winter
to keep things right.

Our Orchard in Flag Hill

I miss walking down the lane
feeling a southwest wind breathing,
my dad driving the hay wagon
as I traipse my way to the apple orchard.
Hundreds of apple trees were planted
by my father fifteen years ago.
Over full green fields, trees thrust out crimson buds
and pink blossoms suffused sweet perfume.

In the orchard I listened to the convention
of blue birds, my eyes blinking;
one male with bright orange breast clung
to the cavity entrance of the nest box defying
house wrens and English sparrows
from taking over.

Here and there, as I stooped down to gather
some blue Quaker ladies and meadow buttercups,
a peacock butterfly passed over my hands.

In October, fall palpitated on the scene
as arbor of trees yielded a wealth of golden
and crimson apples. Turned out of the house,
my sisters and I gathered bushels of apples
climbing the spreading branches.
The fragrant sweet scent lured the hawk
moth and bumble bee pollinators.
This memory sharp as a blade
on my father's whetstone wheel.

Sea Turtle Breaking Through

Swimming and pushing hard
through the daily tightness,
teasing oxygen from the ocean
my loggerhead turtle is determined
to gain mileage and not take forever
to get safely ashore.
She must be vigilant
watch out for predators
and escape from a sea lion
to find a home
on a sandy beach and look
for a safe place to lay her eggs.

She did not burrow like a clam
on the bottom of the ocean.
Instead, she smashes
through the roaring blue-green waves.
With her bright determined body,
she is strong of heart,
breaking through all setbacks,
knowing time is running out.
If she arrives on the sand
she will haul
herself up the beach at night
and lay her fragile eggs.

Lakewood Ranch — Another World

Imagine a landscape with tall trees of cypress
bearing circles of feathery branches.
A dense grove of small and large palms
surround an Olympic-size pool.
Oak trees along pathways are draped
with gray moss and lichen.
The air smells fragrant
from the purple- blue- pink hydrangeas
and kwanza cherry trees that bloom in all seasons.
Behind every villa, a made lake, bright and glittering,
reflects the translucent blue vividness of the sky.
One pure white egret on the shore
and a curious alligator pops up with eyes-bulging,
In the parking lot I thrill to watch
a family of sandhill cranes; mother,
father and two babies stretch their wings and leap into the air.
All around the landscape from dawn to dusk,
male and female landscapers swelter through yellow jackets,
woven hats and black boots.
In the summer a rain shower every day cleans the air
Far away a thundering cloud turns the blue sky to grey.
More birds are gathering, mostly mockingbirds
singing spirited songs and adding new ones
to their elaborate repertoire.

Carol Leavitt Altieri was born in Boston, Massachusetts and grew up on a farm in East Andover, New Hampshire during the Great Depression (1936–1950) which lasted much longer there. The echoes of early life on the farm and the natural world enhance her poetry. She continues to explore all aspects of nature on the Shoreline of Connecticut.

Other poems are interwoven with travels in the United States and other countries: Brazil, British Isles, Canada, Costa Rica, France, Mexico, New Zealand, Soviet Union, Spain, Venezuela and Yugoslavia.

Carol has completed graduate study and was awarded the Certificate of Advanced Study at Wesleyan University in 2001 after receiving a Masters Degree in English and a Sixth Year Degree in Educational Leadership, at Southern Connecticut State University. While there, she received Graduate Poet of the Year.

Recipient of an English Speakers Union Scholarship, Carol has studied English literature and culture at the University of London and accepted in Yale/New Haven Teachers Institute for six years.

A member of the Guilford Poets Guild, she is now retired. She has published seven previous books of poetry: *The Isinglass River, In Beijing there are no Dawn Redwoods, The Jade Bower, Still Brooding on a Strong Branch, Chronicles of Humans With Nature, Parables of Passages, Hiking the Rugged Shore* and now *Breaking Through.*

She participates in nature conservation and takes workshops in poetry writing. She enjoys her grandchildren, hiking, bird watching and reading natural history, poetry and creative nonfiction. She recently won a Connecticut Green Circle Award for Environmental activism — as she worked ten years as an activist preserving the shoreline from over development. During the pandemic, she explores the Hammonasset Beach. She is moving to Lakewood Ranch for six months each winter.